MAGNIFICENT
TIFFANY WINDOWS
COLORING BOOK

LOUIS COMFORT TIFFANY

RENDERED FOR COLORING BY
MARTY NOBLE

DOVER PUBLICATIONS, INC.
MINEOLA, NEW YORK

Louis Comfort Tiffany (1848–1933) was a bold pioneer of modern design. Originally trained as a painter, Tiffany loved the unique qualities of glass and was intrigued by the idea that glasswork could be functional as well as beautiful. Tiffany began experimenting with glass in 1875; by the 1890s he had produced an inimitable type of glass that he called *favrile*—it was iridescent, freely textured, and often combined with metal alloys for shimmering effects. Influenced by William Morris, whose work had launched the Arts and Crafts movement, Tiffany wished to render figures in stained glass windows without the use of brushwork. In his exquisite stained glass, he demonstrates an arts-and-crafts conscience in his respect for materials, and a desire to transform the way Americans regarded the function of art in the home.

Set in locations from New York, New England, and Pennsylvania to Michigan and Minnesota, among others, these thirty-one magnificent Tiffany windows will inspire you to use coloring media to recreate the charm and beauty of the original glasswork. And the perforated, unbacked pages make displaying your finished work easy!

Copyright

Copyright © 2008, 2017 by Dover Publications, Inc.
All rights reserved.

Bibliographical Note

Magnificent Tiffany Windows Coloring Book, first published by
Dover Publications, Inc., in 2017, contains thirty plates (Plate #4 revised)
from *Color Your Own Tiffany Windows* (Dover, 2008); also included is a
new plate (#31), created specially for this edition.

International Standard Book Number

ISBN-13: 978-0-486-81492-6
ISBN-10: 0-486-81492-0

Manufactured in the United States by LSC Communications
81492001   2017
www.doverpublications.com

1. "Antony van Corlear, Trumpeter of New Amsterdam"

Historical portrait window designed by Howard Pyle

The Colonial Club, New York City, c. 1896.

2. Landscape window (detail), part of a ten-panel window

Commissioned by Richard B. Mellon for his house

Pittsburgh, Pennsylvania, 1908–12.

3. Landscape window

Fenway Gate

Boston, Massachusetts, c. 1912.

4. "Tree of Life"

The Allen Parkhill Northrop Memorial Window (detail)

Designed by his daughter, Alice Northrop

Reformed Church

Flushing, New York, 1903.

5. "Holy City"

The John Webster Oothout Memorial Window

Third Presbyterian Church

Rochester, New York, c. 1902.

6. Domestic floral window

Date and location unknown.

7. "Christ Blessing Little Children"

The Amelia and Foster Barrett Memorial Window

Christ Episcopal Church

Greenwich, Connecticut, c. 1900.

8. The Margaret Standart Watson Memorial Window

Central Presbyterian Church (now the Westminster Presbyterian)

Auburn, New York, c. 1900.

9. The Frederic Henry Betts Memorial Window

St. Andrew's Dune Church

Southampton, Long Island, New York, c. 1906.

10. The Redfield Proctor Memorial Diptych Window

(left panel detail)

Union Church

Proctor, Vermont, c. 1909.

11. The Redfield Proctor Memorial Diptych Window

(right panel detail)

Union Church

Proctor, Vermont, c. 1909.

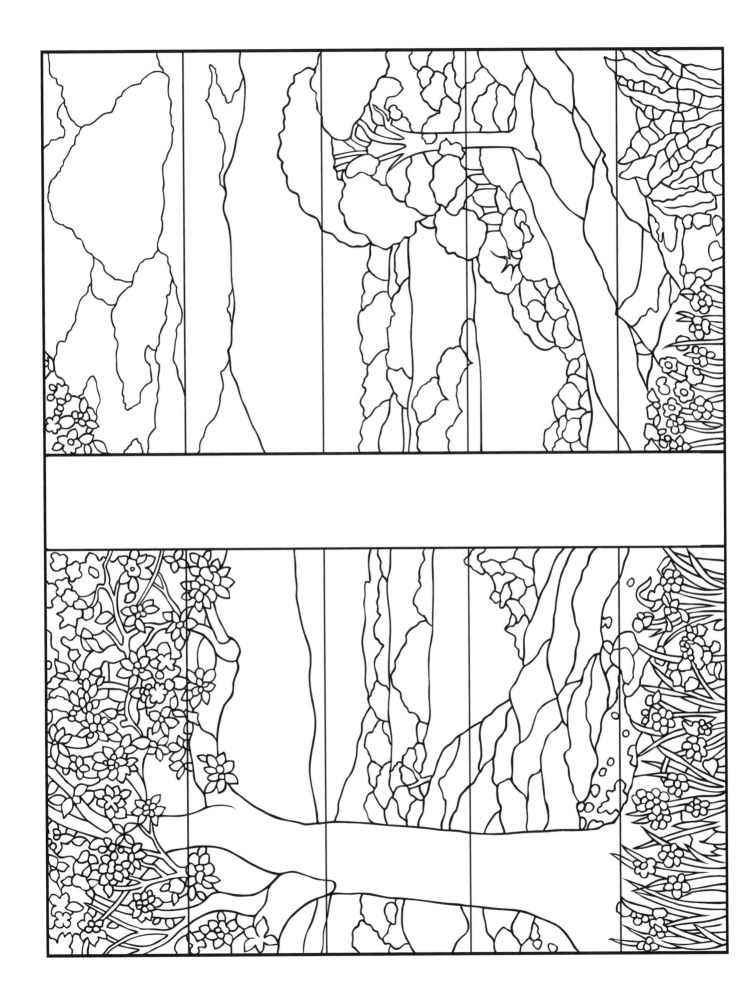

12. The Minnie E. Proctor Memorial Diptych Window

Union Church

Proctor, Vermont, 1928.

13. The Frank Memorial Window

Date unknown.

14. Landscape window

Date unknown.

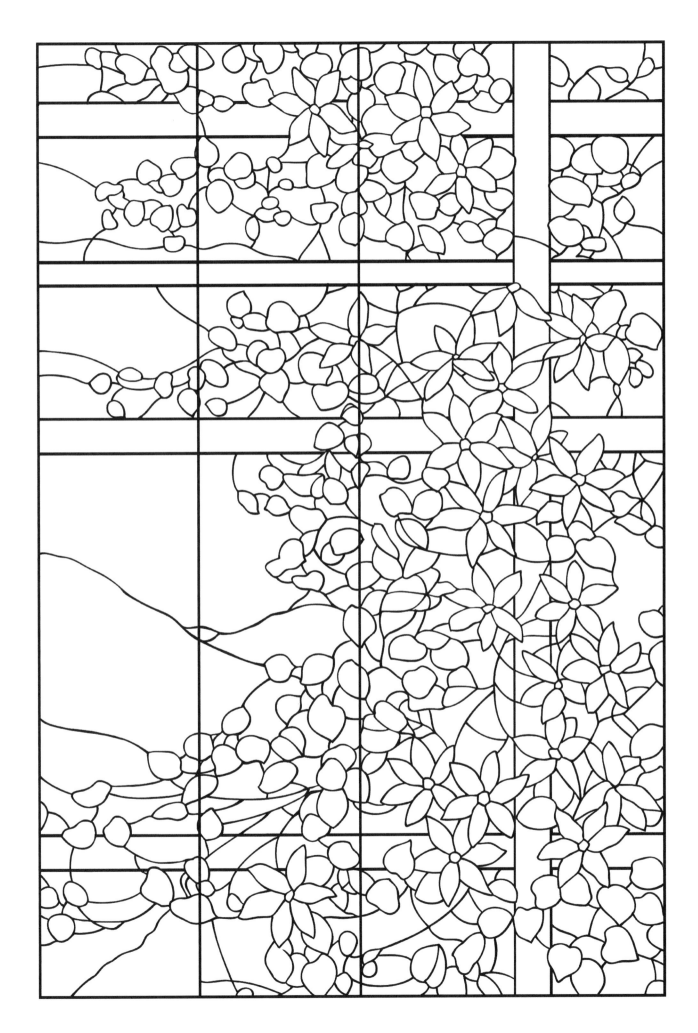

15. Floral skylight (detail)

Fenway Gate

Boston, Massachusetts, c. 1912.

16. Peacock window

Private residence

New England, c. 1910.

17. Landscape window

Date unknown.

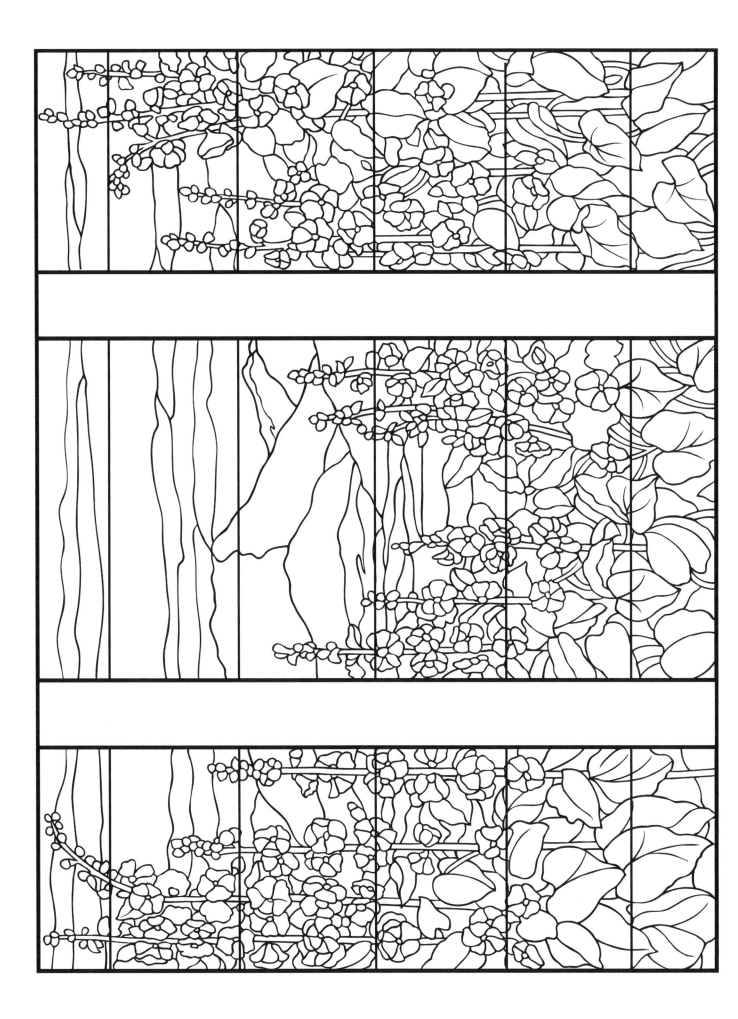

18. Domestic triptych window with hollyhocks

in a landscape

Date unknown.

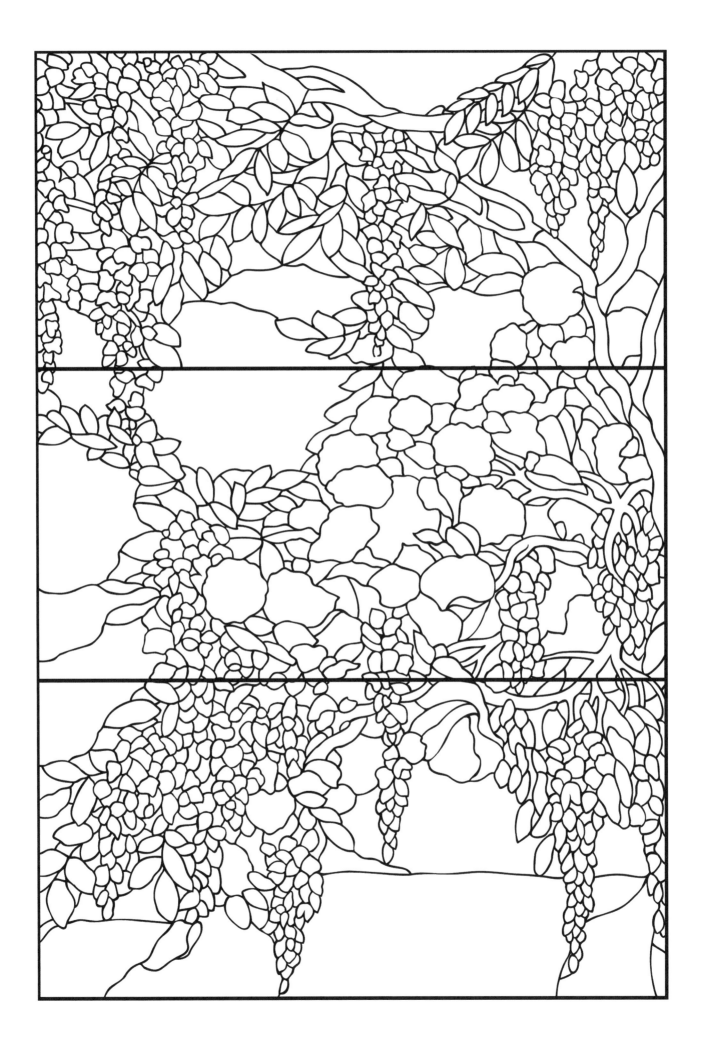

19. Domestic window

Date unknown.

20. The Charles A. Duncan and William G. Hegardt Memorial Window

Pilgrim Congregational Church

Duluth, Minnesota, c. 1924.

21. Rose window

Laurelton Hall

Long Island, New York, 1906.

22. Figure window of young woman amongst foliage

Date unknown.

23. Landscape window in mansion for Webb Horton

Middletown, New York, 1902.

24. Domestic window (detail)

Captain Joseph R. Delamar House

New York City, c. 1912.

25. "Peace" (detail)

The Ann Eliza Brainerd Smith Memorial Landscape Window

The First Congregational Church

St. Albans, Vermont, c. 1905.

26. "Come unto Me"

The Widener Memorial

St. Stephen's Church

Philadelphia, Pennsylvania, date unknown.

27. Window on stairway landing

Wayne Community College

Detroit, Michigan, date unknown.

28. "Fawn at a Stream" (detail)

Triptych memorial window, c. 1922.

29. "Parrots on Branches"

Domestic window, private collection, 1893.

30. "View of Oyster Bay" (detail)

Wisteria landscape window designed for the home of

William C. Skinner

New York City, 1908.

31. "Magnolia and Wisteria"

Sarah Fay Sumner Memorial Window

Agnes Northrop, designer

First Reformed Church

Albany, New York, 1912.